Falaise Castle
William the Conqueror's birthplace

Catherine DUCHEMIN
Charlotte LAPICHE
Benoît PANOZZO

OREP
EDITIONS

Aerial view from the southwest; the castle overlooking the town. Falaise Town Council.

The origins of the town and the castle

Located 20 miles to the south of Caen, Falaise and its castle lie at the junction between two natural regions: to the north, a fertile limestone sediment plain stretching to the sea and comprising the Caen plain - to the south, the eastern extremity of the Armorican Massif whose sandstone and schist escarpment provide the bedrock for the castle and the walled town.

Today, the castle forms an irregular enclosure, facing northwest to southeast, embracing the form of the terrain on which it was built. The rampart, flanked with fifteen towers, encloses a total surface area of around one and a half hectares, separated by a ditch and an upper and lower courtyard.

The ensemble is dominated to the northwest by the mass of the three keeps that occupy the least accessible part of the rocky outcrop.

Although proof of human presence in the area around Falaise dates back to 60,000 years BC, its permanent occupation began during the Neolithic Age (circa 5,000 years BC). Roadways which facilitated trade, along with scattered settlements, began to develop throughout the region with the arrival of the Celts as from the 5th century BC. Several traces of occupation around Falaise also date from the Gallo-Roman period (30 years BC to the year 400).
As from the 9th century, the region was undermined by the Viking incursions. Henceforth, the rocky spur may well have been endowed with an early fortification aimed at protecting against such attacks. Yet no proof – be it archaeological or documentary – offers confirmation of this. Falaise would appear to have been born from the establishment of a castle by the first Dukes of Normandy. A structure that is believed to have favoured the growth of a castle town. Trace of an older city may lie under the present-day town; however, the density of its constructions render any such identification a difficult task.

Normandy was founded in the year 911, when Charles the Simple, King of the Franks, conceded to the Viking chief Rollo a vast territory stretching across either bank of the Seine estuary. This principality, which corresponded roughly to the present-day départements of Seine-Maritime and Eure, rapidly stretched westwards to include the region around Falaise as from the year 933. The site reunited many favourable conditions for the establishment of a fortified town: the presence of a rocky outcrop encircled by two waterways and enabling the control of the crossroads between two strategic routes – the first running from north to south and linking the sea with Anjou, and the second running from east to west and linking the Île-de-France region with Brittany.

The physiognomy of the original castle, most probably built under Richard I, is unknown. Yet a recent archaeological study of the ramparts revealed that the present-day enclosure includes large sections of the original wall. This recent discovery confirms the fact that Falaise was home to one of the very first stone castles in Normandy. In the 10th and 11th centuries, stone was typically used for princely fortifications; those of lesser lords being essentially made of wood and earth.

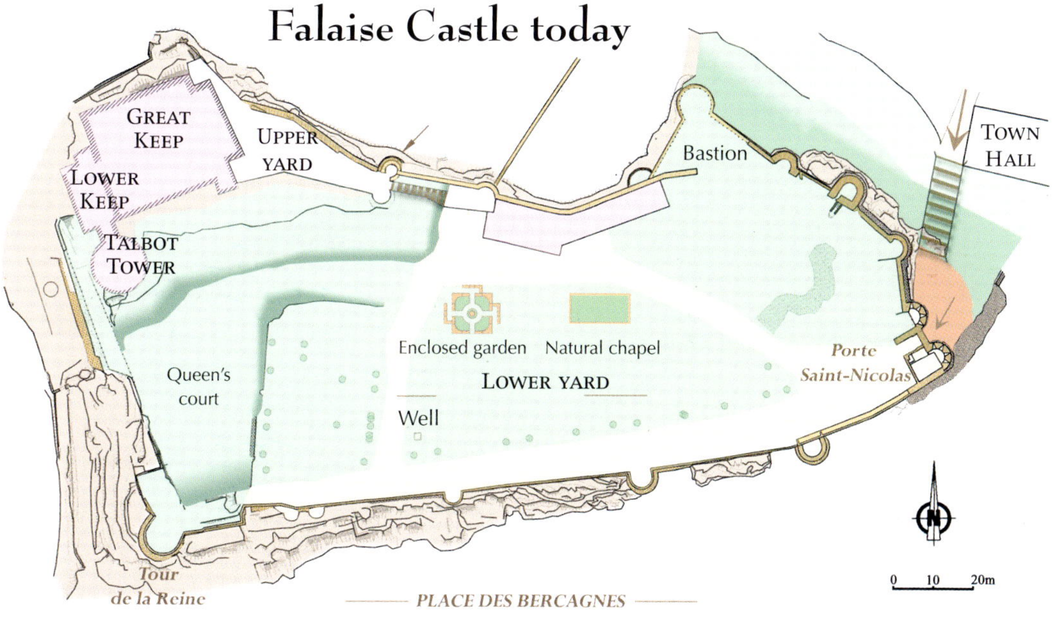

Location map. Falaise Town Council.

The keeps: southwest aerial view.
Photograph F. Trouillet / Town of Falaise.

Chronology

5th century: construction of a fortified castle made of stone on the rocky outcrop overlooking the River Ante.

1027: Falaise castle was Robert the Magnificent's favourite place of residence.

Christmas 1027: birth of William in Falaise.

1123: construction of the Great Keep and alterations to the castle enclosure by William's son, Henry I Beauclerc.

1159: Henry II Plantagenet, Henry Beauclerc's grandson, held his Christmas court in Falaise, accompanied by his wife, Eleanor of Aquitaine.

1207: the King of France, Philip Augustus, had the Talbot Tower built and modernised the castle enclosure by building several flanking towers and a fortified gateway at the entrance to the upper courtyard.

1337: onset of the Hundred Years' War.

1418: Falaise was besieged by the King of England, Henry V. Start of the English occupation.

1450: the French King Charles VII recaptured the town and its castle from the English.

1590: Henry IV, King of France's troops attacked Falaise, hitherto held by the Catholic League.

The King's modern artillery met with little resistance, easily weakening the castle walls, which were dismantled after his victory.

1790: the Keeps were mercifully spared from destruction.

1803: creation of a school on the site of the former viscount's lodge.

1840: the castle was listed as a Historic Monument by Prosper Mérimée.

1863-1913: major restoration campaigns involving the keeps were undertaken by the architect Victor Ruprich-Robert, followed by Gustave Ruprich-Robert and Trolonge.

1944: the choir of the St. Nicholas chapel and the school buildings were destroyed by bombs. However, the keeps were left almost intact.

1948: archaeological excavation at the foot of the Great Keep under the auspices of Dr Doranlo: the vestiges of the forebuilding were discovered.

1980: Falaise Town Council planned to rehabilitate the keeps. The project was entrusted to the chief architect of Historic Monuments, Bruno Decaris.

1986-1987: restoration work on the three keeps. The castle was re-opened to the public in 1997.

2003-2004: restoration of the upper courtyard by the chief architect of Historic Monuments, Daniel Lefèvre.

2007-2011: campaign to restore the castle enclosure directed by Daniel Lefèvre. The campaign aimed at recreating the site's defensive role.

Scale model of a 10th and 11th century castle mound.

Spring 1027, Arlette arrives at the castle.
Illustration by P. Noir / Falaise Town Council.

Falaise and William the Conqueror

The town of Falaise is renowned particularly as being the birthplace of the most famous of the Norman Dukes, William the Conqueror.

Spring 1027: Robert, known as "the Magnificent", who was Richard II, Duke of Normandy's brother, resided in his castle in the town of Falaise; he was around seventeen years old. Robert Wace, a 12th century poet from Jersey, tells us the rest of his story in *Le Roman de Rou* (circa 1155-1160): 'The Duke had gone to Falaise where he stayed several times. He had loved a young girl there, named Arlette, whose father was a burgher from the town. She was still very young, and the duke found her beautiful and charming...' Arlette became the young lord's concubine. A little later... 'When they had, for a long time, taken great care of each other (I wish to say no more of the pleasures a man may take with his lady friend), the young girl fell asleep and the noble baron lying alongside her did nothing to push her away. When she had slept for a while, following a vision she had had, she gave a doleful cry and a shudder that the nobleman could feel. He asked her the reason for her angst, "Lord," she replied, "I know not, unless it is because of the dream I had. I saw a tree emerge from my body and grow very high towards the sky. Of the shadow it cast around it, all Normandy was covered." - "That will be good," he said, "if it pleases God." He comforted her and drew her towards him. It is by this very Arlette that a son named William was born.'

Arlette's Fountain.
Early 20th century postcard.
Pays de Falaise Media library.

Simplified genealogy of the Norman Dukes: from Rollo to William the Conqueror.

Source: François Neveux, *La Normandie des ducs aux rois - Xᵉ-XIIᵉ siècles*, Ed. Ouest France Université.

1 **Rollo**
(911-932)

2 **William Longsword**
(932-942)

3 **Richard I "the Fearless"**
(942-996)

Emma

1 ~ **Aethelred II**
King of England
(978-1015)

2 ~ **Canute the Great**
King of England
(1016-1035)

Edward the Confessor
King of England
(1042-1066)

Harthacanute
King of England
(1040-1042)

4 **Richard II "the Good"**
(996-1026)

5 **Richard III**
(1026-1027)

6 **Robert the Magnificent**
(1027-1035)

Statue of William the Conqueror on horseback located in Place Guillaume le Conquérant, opposite the Town Hall. Falaise Town Council

~ **Herleva** ~ **Herluin de Conteville**

William the Bastard
Duke of Normandy (1035-1087)
King of England (1066-1087)

Odo
Bishop of Bayeux

Robert
Count of Mortain

"I dreamt that a tree was emerging from my body".
Illustration by E. Cerisier.

1047: the Battle of Val-ès-Dunes.
Illustration by E. Cerisier.

Irn 1035, Duke Robert surprised his close circles by announcing his planned pilgrimage to Jerusalem. Before he left, he gathered his vassals, laymen and clergymen in Fécamp and he presented his young son William to them as his rightful heir. They all swore loyalty to the child, who was aged just 7 years. The same year, Robert died on his return journey. William became Duke of Normandy, but many lords questioned his right to such a title, creating unrest throughout the duchy. In 1046, a plot was devised while William was staying in Valognes. Warned of the imminent attack a few minutes before his assailants arrived, he fled and rode to Falaise to seek a safe haven within his castle.

The following year, William had no choice but to take up arms and to challenge the rebellious noblemen. With help from his suzerain, King Henry I of France, he won a decisive battle at Val-ès-Dunes near Caen. His rights now firmly established, he could concentrate on developing his duchy. Around the year 1050, William married Matilda, the daughter of his most powerful European neighbour, Baldwin V, the Count of Flanders. Their union reinforced the prosperity of the Norman principality.

Portrait of William. Illustration by E. Cerisier.

1057: the Battle of Varaville. Illustration by E. Cerisier.

When the King of England, Edward the Confessor, chose William to succeed him, the event was for a long time to disrupt the political balance in the already insecure kingdom of France. When Edward died on the 5th of January 1066, Harold, his brother-in-law, was crowned king of England. The Duke of Normandy then organised a vast military expedition to cross the English Channel and to take back the crown. In just a few months, he succeeded the feat of reuniting 15,000 men, 4,000 horses and all the necessary equipment for a thousand ships, and he landed in England.

The confrontation between Harold and William took place in October 1066, near the town of Hastings. The deadly battle was to last one day. It was only late in the afternoon that the Normans and their Breton, French and Flemish allies forced the English resistance to yield. King Harold, already wounded in the eye by an arrow, was killed, leading to his army's rout.

Arriving in England. Illustration by E. Cerisier.

Talbot Tower and Great Keep seen from the lower courtyard. Falaise Town Council.

The castle's evolution over the centuries

After subjecting the city of London, William chose Christmas Day 1066 to be crowned in the brand new church of Westminster, where his cousin Edward the Confessor was laid to rest. William's later years were darkened by his rebellious son Robert Curthose, and by the death of his wife, Matilda, in 1083. Seriously wounded during an expedition against the King of France, William was taken to Rouen, where he died on the 9th of September 1087. Although the affairs of the duchy and the kingdom of England had gradually distanced William from Falaise, he had always maintained great esteem for his birthplace and its inhabitants' unfailing loyalty.

The castle in the 12th century

Upon William's death, his sons Robert "Curthose", William "Rufus" and Henry "Beauclerc" fought for over twenty years over his legacy, until Henry finally gained the upper hand in 1106. In order to reorganise his duchy and to seal his frontiers, he undertook a major campaign to improve his existing castles and to build new ones. As such, he had Falaise Castle almost totally rebuilt around the year 1123. The ramparts were partially razed and painstakingly rebuilt. A massive rectangular keep was erected at the summit of the rocky outcrop. It was a reproduction of those built by the Normans in England, following the conquest of 1066.

In the foreground, the hoarding represented using augmented reality.
Falaise Town Council / Normandy Productions.

The Great Keep in Falaise is a dense rectangular tower whose walls are reinforced with flat buttresses. It measures 87 feet long by 75 feet wide, reaching a height of over 66 feet. Its walls are of an average depth of 11 feet. At the time of its construction, its different levels were floored with planks of wood and its roof frame probably covered with shingle. The Keep's only entrance, located in the east wall, is on the first floor. It was accessed via an outside staircase that was integrated within a defensive forebuilding. Since disappeared, the forebuilding and the staircase are now evoked by means of a modern reconstruction that recalls the defensive role of the original access. The ground floor was almost blind to the outside world, hence protecting it from intrusion. It was used to store provisions, weapons and ammunition. It also housed a kitchen, which may have been equipped with a stove, and a cistern.

The first floor of the keep included vast lodgings for the duke and part of his court during his visits to Falaise. It was arranged in three distinct living areas, according to the customary organisation of 12th century seigniorial residences: it included the *aula*, a public ceremonial room used for representation and official functions - political assemblies, hearings, pleas, welcoming guests or even festivities. A partition wall separates the *aula* from the *camera*. This private bedroom was more than just a simple place to sleep. It very probably comprised the private apartments of the lord and his close circle. Finally, adjoining to the *camera* there is the *capella*, a private chapel housed within a salient buttress on the keep's south-east angle. Served by the ducal chaplains, it offered the duke and his family all the comfort and convenience of a private church at home, during a period when religious practice was an integral part of everyday life. Its architecture is of elegant sobriety and is a fine example of Norman-Roman style.

The Anglo-Norman keeps

Scale model of the Tower of London. © Tapisserie de Bayeux.

After 1066, the Normans' priority was to assert their power in England, among a Saxon population that was both hostile and in far greater numbers. They covered the kingdom with castles. These fortified operational bases kept the population at bay and symbolised the Norman domination. Many of these fortresses, initially made of wood and earth, were rapidly reinforced with a quadrangular stone keep. The most famous among them is undoubtedly the Tower of London, the construction of which began in the 1070s. Under one roof, it offered all the commodities of a palace and the safety of a refuge in the case of an uprising. The sheer dimension of these tower-residences, also referred to as palace-keeps, symbolised the domination of the Norman aristocracy over Saxon England.

Rochester Keep.
Photograph by R. Turner.

The roof level was used as a lookout and to ensure the castle's nearby defence. The top of the walls was very probably crowned with a crenellated parapet, which was perhaps equipped with hoarding (exterior wooden galleries enabling projectiles to be thrown to the foot of the walls). The different levels were reached by means of stairs built within the walls which also integrated annexe rooms.

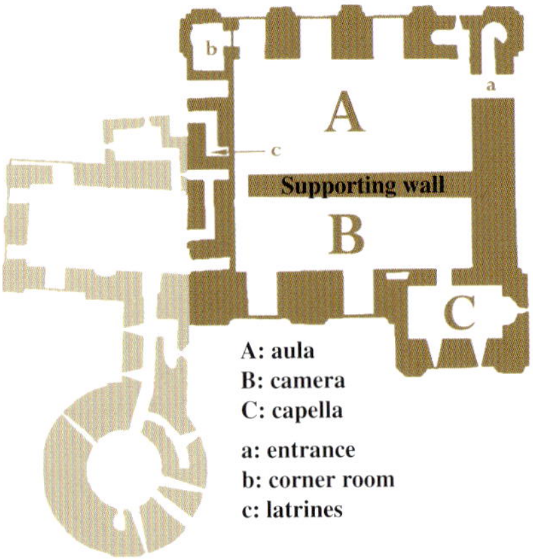

Residential floor of the Great Keep.

Living conditions in the Great Keep

The residential floor was an ostentatious area flaunting the status of its proprietor, finely decorated and with comfortable furnishings. The walls were covered with whitewash, a material that was renowned for its hygienic qualities. It was most probably originally adorned with decorative paintings.

The keep was remarkably comfortable compared to the period's standard living conditions. The residential floor's twin windows adorned with sculpted capitals offered a largely sufficient input of natural light. The latrines offered the keep's inhabitants a certain degree of hygiene. The fireplace which can be admired in the *camera*, largely restored in the 19th century, may well be an original feature. The heating system was completed with open hearths and braziers. The windows were closed by means of interior wooden shutters. Glass – which was very costly in the 12th century

The *capella* in augmented reality.
Falaise Town Council / Normandy Productions.

The *capella* today.
Photograph by M. Dilys / Falaise Town Council.

- was not even used to close the richest of dwellings. It was specifically reserved for use in churches. Yet, it could be satisfactorily replaced by oiled or waxed fabric, or even by animal bladder skins stretched out over a frame. Fabric wall coverings were hung on the walls to improve the lodging's insulation. The floor was generally covered with natural foliage (straw, fresh grass, bulrush) or matting. Over and above natural sunlight, oil lamps provided further lighting to the interior.

The purpose of the *camera* changed depending on the time of day; it was in turn used as a dining room, a living room, a workplace, a bedroom... Intimacy was obtained by using the areas behind curtains which were used to partition the room. There was very little furniture. It was essentially functional and easy to transport for it accompanied the lord's itinerant court from one residence to another: removable tables comprised of planks placed on trestles, seats, benches and stools, chests for storage and a few beds used exclusively for distinguished guests. Servants and soldiers generally slept on simple straw mattresses placed directly on the floor and in collective sleeping quarters. Thus, the *aula* served as a dormitory in the evening.

The *aula* today. Photograph by M. Dilys / Falaise Town Council.

The *camera* today. Photograph by M. Dilys / Falaise Town Council.

The castle under the Plantagenets

In the second half of the 12th century, a new building was added alongside the west facade of the Great Keep. It was based on the same principle but of smaller size (46 feet long by 33 feet wide and 46 feet high). This new building offered two advantages: far more efficient defence of the western front and an extension to the lodgings. Its sophisticated architecture clearly asserted its princely and royal status. The upper floor hall was equipped with a large fireplace, the refractory brick back wall of which improved its efficiency. Light was brought to the hall by means of wide carved windows which offered maximum natural sunlight all year round. It comprised a bright and harmoniously proportioned living area.

Built under the Plantagenet reign, the Small Keep bears witness to the peak of Anglo-Norman power. By way of legacies and matrimonial alliances, Henry II Plantagenet, William the Conqueror's great grandson, found himself at the head of an estate stretching from the confines of Scotland to the foothills of the Pyrenees, as from 1154. As a great administrator and indefatigable explorer, Henry II continuously travelled the length and breadth of his possessions.

Window with window seats and cannon holes added in the early 15th century.
Illustration by B. Decaris / Falaise Town Council.

His trips to Normandy – and to Falaise in particular – were frequent. A rectangular turret, accessible from the residential hall, was added to the north wall of the Small Keep. Its purpose is unknown, yet the most probable theory is that it served as a latrine tower.

Henry II and his sons, Richard the Lionheart and John Lackland, invested vast sums of money to maintain and improve Falaise Castle. Receipts dating from the period only evoke work "on the fortifications" without offering any further indication as to the detail of such intervention. Nevertheless, archaeology has unveiled that the first towers that flanked the castle rampart were built during this period.

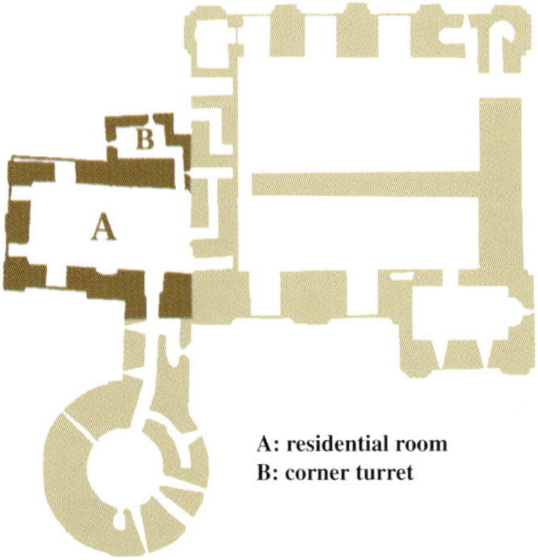

Site plan of the Small Keep.

Built during the reign of the Plantagenets, the Small Keep is located at the rocky outcrop's extremity. Adjoining the Great Keep, this elegant construction also associated both a defensive and a residential purpose. Falaise Town Council.

Residential room in the Small Keep: the recreated furnishings depict the omnipresence of colour in noble medieval residences.
Photograph by M. Dilys / Falaise Town Council.

Detail of one of the fireplace capitals. Photograph by M. Dilys / Falaise Town Coun

The Norman Duke-Kings descended from William

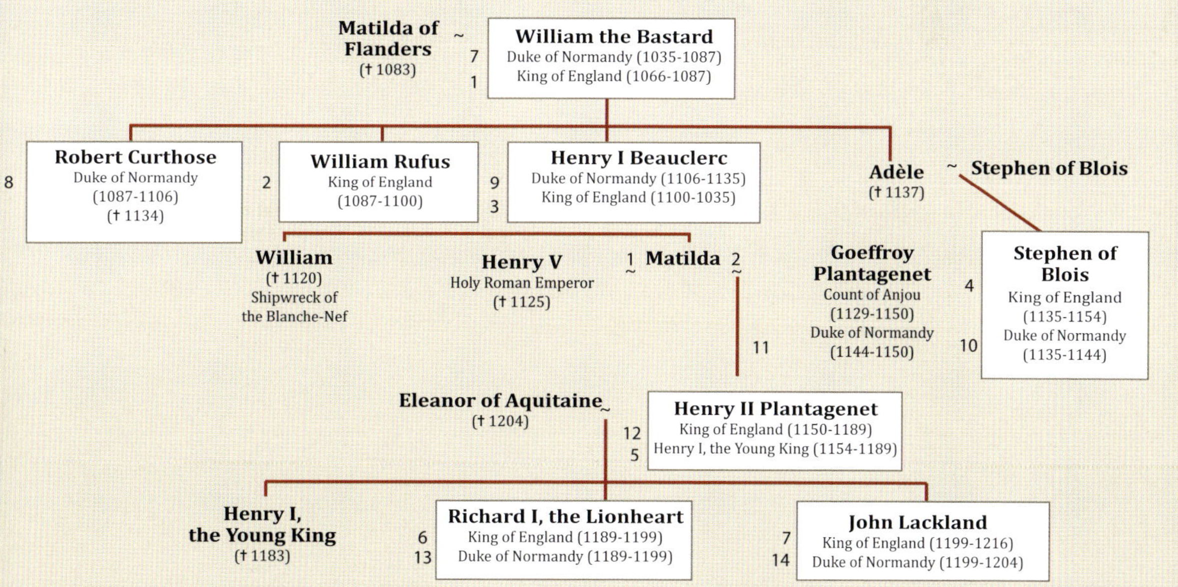

The castle in the 13th century

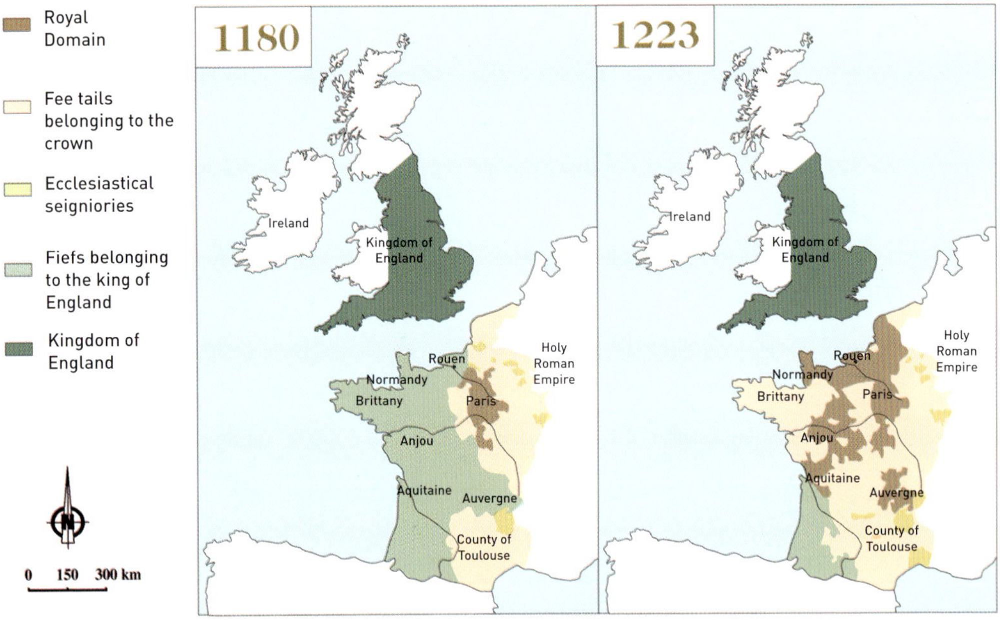

The expansion of the royal domain during the reign of Philip Augustus (1180-1223).

In the early 13th century, the King of France, Philip II Augustus, put a permanent end to the threat posed on his kingdom by the territorial power of the English Kings, who were his vassals on the Continent. He seized a timely opportunity to pronounce the confiscation of the fiefs belonging to the English King John Lackland, most of which he had annexed. Normandy was conquered in its entirety in June 1204 and was incorporated within the royal domain. Philip Augustus made major alterations to Falaise Castle. He applied the cautious principles of defensive architecture set down by the master builders at his service. A fortified gateway was built to reinforce the defence of the upper courtyard. In 1207, he had a large cylindrical tower built next to the two Romanesque keeps: the Talbot Tower.

Around the mid 13th century, the surface area of the castle enclosure was extended westwards via the massive addition of back-fill leading to the creation of the present-day

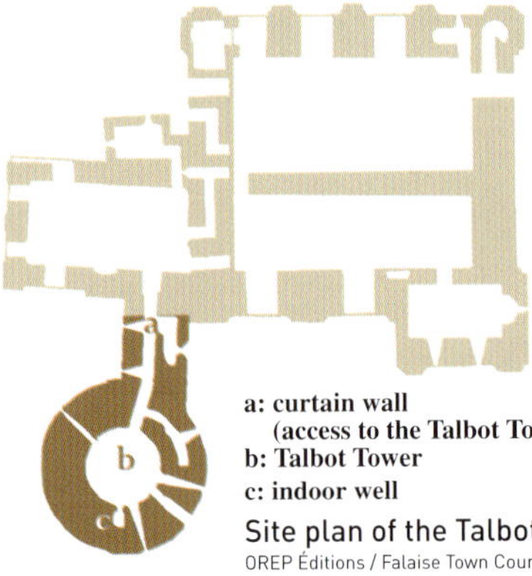

a: curtain wall (access to the Talbot Tower)
b: Talbot Tower
c: indoor well

Site plan of the Talbot Tower.
OREP Éditions / Falaise Town Council.

The upper courtyard, following restoration of the fortified gateway from 2001 to 2004 by the Chief Architect of Historic Monuments, Daniel Lefèvre.
Photograph by M. Dilys / Falaise Town Council.

Cour de la Reine (Queen's courtyard). This extension, which required large-scale work, was justified by the will to bring the Talbot Tower within the ramparts. Finally, Philip Augustus, or his immediate successors, improved the town and the castle ramparts by adding semi-circular towers designed to efficiently flank the curtain walls.

Another example of 13th century architecture – the Porte des Cordeliers gateway. Built under Philip Augustus, it once secured the castle enclosure from the town. Falaise Town Council.

The Talbot Tower

The Talbot Tower is a master-tower quite typical of Philip Augustus's reign. Based on an easily reproducible standard model adopted throughout the kingdom, these towers offered solid defensive enclaves whilst constituting a striking symbol of royal power. The present-day tower measures 115 feet in height, for a diameter of 46 feet at its base. Its circular shape limited the creation of dead angles, which were the major weakness of quadrangular keeps. Its walls - extremely thick and carefully bonded - offered excellent resistance to projectiles. Its full base in the truncated cone discouraged any attempt at sapping. The tower comprised six levels, excluding the summit, with alternating stone ribbed vaults and wooden floors. The former reinforced the overall structure and protected from fire, whilst the latter lightened the construction. The lowest level was blind. It was used as a cellar and may also have occasionally served as a dungeon. It can only be accessed via an opening in the centre of the upper level flooring. This opening has since been condemned by a sealed slab. A well dug within the depth of the tower wall offered a supply of fresh water. On each floor, a circular opening enabled heavy loads to be winched up. These openings very probably also enabled orders and instructions to be rapidly transmitted from one tower level to another. Light and ventilation were provided by simple slits which also reinforced safety. They were not loopholes per se, for short-range defence - firing arrows, dropping projectiles – was conducted from the keep roof. The larger windows on the upper floors were added after the 13th century. The tower was heightened in the 15th century during English occupation over the Hundred Years' War. This extension enabled the creation of two further residential levels, separated by a wooden floor, but which have since disappeared. The architectural quality of its comfort facilities – fireplaces and mullion windows – leads us to suppose that these rooms were reserved for use by important garrison officers.

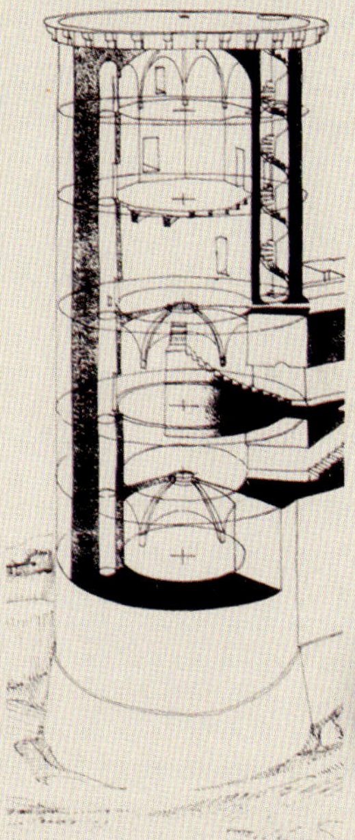

Cross-section of the Talbot Tower before restoration in 1986. The alternating floors and stone vault ceilings comprising the tower's different levels can clearly be seen. Illustration by B. Decaris / Falaise Town Council.

The Talbot Tower. Falaise Town Council.

The Hundred Years' War (1337 – 1453)

The Hundred Years' War began in 1337, with Edward III of England's claim to the French throne. Attention to the castle's maintenance had been considerably neglected during the long peaceful period which immediately preceded the conflict. However, from the very start of the war, the royal administrative bodies immediately became aware of the necessity to return the kingdom's castles to a sufficiently defensive state. Major work was undertaken on the fortress. The ramparts were heightened, the gates and masonry were reinforced, crenellation were repaired and the stronghold was henceforth sufficiently manned and equipped. The castle also had its own artillery: two "engines of war" capable of launching heavy stone projectiles (evidence of which dates from 1364) and several cannons, first mentioned in 1380.

During the first decades of the conflict, the town suffered no direct attack. However, various troops of local belligerents or pillagers driven by misery brought a reign of insecurity over the surrounding countryside. To add to these misfortunes, the plague was rife and heavy taxes were levied to finance the war. The economy had declined and the town's prosperity was severely shaken. On the 1st of August 1417, Henry V, King of England, landed in Trouville and launched a campaign to totally conquer Normandy. His army reached the walls of Falaise on the 4th of September the same year. The town's inhabitants and the castle garrison put up valiant resistance to the English. The city only fell in January 1418; the castle surrendered a month later. The English occupation lasted thirty-two years. Henry V had the fortifications, sorely damaged by the siege, repaired. He also adapted them to suit new warfaring techniques: certain firing holes in the enclosure towers were modified and others were created to integrate the use of firearms to the defensive system. As from 1431, the military and political situation turned permanently in favour of the French King Charles VII. In 1449, he undertook to reconquer Normandy. He laid siege to Falaise on the 6th of July 1450. The English were driven out on the 22nd of July.

The town of Falaise recaptured by Charles VII in 1450.
Miniature taken from Les Vigiles de Charles VII, circa 1480.
BnF (French National Library), Ref: ms. Fr. 5054, fo 202 v.

The siege of Falaise in 1027 by Richard III against his brother Robert the Magnificent. Although the siege portrayed here took place in the 11th century, the artist sought inspiration in the castles and equipment from his own period.
Miniature take from Chroniques de Normandie, 15th century,
BnF (French National Library). Ref: ms. Fr. 2623, fo 40.

The medieval defences on the castle outskirts

Since at least the 12th century, locks and water canals regulated the waters of the River Marescot (today underground), at the time

Orders from Charles V in 1368 and 1369

Preserved archives dating from the 14th century are abundant. They offer an excellent insight into the measures which were taken to defend the kingdom. Charles V, in particular, multiplied his defensive instructions. In 1368, he ordered the Viscount of Falaise to dismantle the defensive features of any fortified churches and abbeys and to transfer their supplies and their goods to the viscounty's castles. In brief, to apply a scorched earth policy "pour que les ennemis s'en puissent avoir ne trouver aucun ne euls avitailler ou prejudice du roy et du païs" (so that the enemy may not use these fortified places and acquire supplies at the expense of the king and his country). The following year, he ordered that the viscount "de jours et de nuis facent faire bon guet" (have a careful watch kept both day and night), and to ensure that the castles within the viscounty be "si garnies de vivres, artillerie et autres choses necessaires a celles forteresses qu'il doie suffire pour ycelles garder» (sufficiently provided with supplies, artillery and other necessary goods to ensure the defence of such fortresses).

Archery and cannon hole created in one of the enclosure towers to enable the use of firearms, first half of the 15th century. Falaise Town Council.

permanently flooding the vast zone located at the foot of the castle's south rampart, today referred to as Place des Bercagnes. This defensive system was continued along the south side of the urban enclosure. The retained water also served as a fishpond. Other defences protected the approach to the castle: dense thorny hedges, stockades and ditches.

Day-to-day life at the castle

Falaise castle was an urban fortification: it dominated and protected the town and fell under the authority of the central power - formerly ducal then royal from 1204 onwards. This power was physically represented by a high-ranking official, the viscount. At the head of a viscounty of which Falaise was the county town, he was entrusted with a number of his overlord's prerogatives: estate management, first instance court rulings, tax collection, maintaining order, defence of his district. The Viscount of Falaise saw the scope of his duties considerably altered from the 11th to the 15th century: occasionally endowed with significant power, the official could also see his role reduced to a strict minimum, or even his position shed. In the 16th century, the viscount's office was merged with that of town mayor. Henceforth, viscounts no longer resided within the castle. As from the English occupation, the fortress was run by a military governor. The position, which gradually became an honorary one after the Middle Ages, was finally scrapped in 1777.

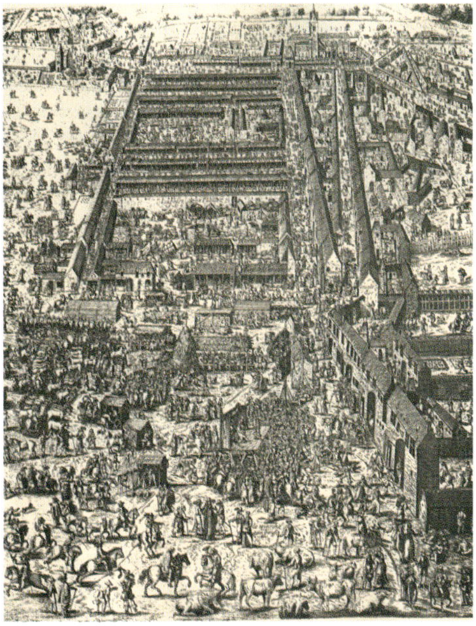

The Guibray Fair in Falaise by François Chauvel (detail). Engraving dating from 1658. Falaise Town Council.

The dwelling kitchen.
Falaise Town Council / Normandy Productions.

An extremely lively lower courtyard

The castle's role was not exclusively defensive. It was as lively in times of peace as it was in times of war. It was indeed a fortress aimed at controlling a given territory, but it was also a seigniorial residence and the seat of his power. These functions required abundant manning throughout the year: an officer representing the Duke of Normandy, then the King of France, together with his family; educated staff in charge of the estate's administration (clerks and lawyers); military staff in charge of defending the stronghold and of policing; servants, in charge of daily chores and of serving distinguished inhabitants; craftsmen to maintain buildings, to produce or repair weapons and day-to-day objects. Thanks to its accounting archives, we know, for example, that at least from the mid 14th century onwards, Falaise Castle was equipped with a forge and a permanent carpentry workshop.

The enclosure interior, where today no medieval construction remains except the three keeps, was, at the time, occupied by a great number of buildings: lodges, barns, stables, cellars and storerooms. They were located in the largest area of the castle enclosure: the lower courtyard. It was home to bustling activity and was organised like a small village. The castle's inhabitants formed a genuine community with its own church: the St. Nicholas Chapel. All of the aforementioned constructions were either built of stone, wooden planks or a combination of both. Their roofs were covered with shingle or tiles.

To every man his castle

The most important administrators were provided with comfortable lodgings within the castle enclosure, knowledge of which we partly owe to preserved work quotes dating from the 14th and 15th centuries and to archaeological excavation. The best-documented lodgings were those of the viscount himself, located at the back of the north rampart since the 12th century - where the present-day visitor's centre stands. Transformed and extended several times, in the Middle Ages, this majestic residential ensemble stretched over around 164 feet in length along the rampart. It comprised rooms devoted to the viscount's duties (hearing room, viscount's writing room, counters), rooms associated with hospitality (viscount's reception room, kitchen), the viscount's and his family's private residence (bedrooms, wardrobe, chapel), together with latrines and a number of outbuildings (storeroom, woodshed, hayloft, stables). According to texts, some of these rooms were adorned with glass windows as early as 1370. The viscount's quarters also had an ornamental garden, mention of which dates from the 14th century. Other buildings included the captain's dwelling, located behind the south rampart near the well, or the bailiff's dwelling, the location of which is unknown, and which boasted facilities comparable to those of the viscount's dwelling. The interior was simple with very little furniture (stools, benches and chairs, chests, tables, beds and dressers). These basic furnishings belonged to the castle's administration, but could be enhanced with the addition of the occupant's personal belongings.

A castle within the town

In times of peace, the castle gates, as those of the town, were left open from dawn to dusk, to enable men and goods to circulate freely. Opening directly onto the city via the Porte Saint-Nicolas gate, the lower courtyard became a quarter in its own right and was an integral part of local life. The castle's civilian and military inhabitants contributed towards the town's vitality, whilst taking advantage of the distractions it offered: shops, inns, steam rooms... Provisions and other supplies which could not be produced within the castle were purchased essentially in town or throughout the surrounding district. Finally, the castle staff was insufficient to cover all the tasks involved in its operation. External workers and craftsmen were regularly called upon for a number of tasks: stonework and roof work, ditch clearing, delivery of supplies, removal of accumulated waste from the enclosure... Through such interaction, the castle contributed considerably towards the town and the area's economic activity.

The town of Falaise flourished during the 12th and 13th centuries, thanks to craft and trade. Linen, hemp and woollen drapery, along with leatherwork contributed to prosperous trading, complemented by agricultural produce from the surrounding countryside. During the 11th and 12th centuries, an annual programme of fairs was initiated. The Guibray fair was to rapidly cast a shadow on all others to become, in the 13th century, one of France's finest. The Norman Conquest and the constitution of the Plantagenet States were also to offer the town a number of new trading opportunities. Falaise benefited, in particular, from the economic privileges granted by the Dukes of Normandy and the Kings of England, then the Kings of France.

The "droit de commune": relative economic and political independence

In 1202, John Lackland, who was always short of money, sold the "droit de commune" to the inhabitants of Falaise: in other words, the right for the inhabitants, under certain conditions, to elect their own mayor and to deal with the town's administration. It also exempted Falaise merchants from all taxes associated with trading with England, with the exception of the city of London. After 1204, Philip Augustus was keen to gain the loyalty of his new subjects and pursued the charters and privileges formerly granted by his predecessors. He added the right to trade, free of taxation, throughout the entire French kingdom, except Mantes, together with an outrageous privilege at a time when the church overtly condemned usury: the right for the people of Falaise to lend money at interest rates reaching up to 99%!

The castle from the Renaissance to the 19th century

The Wars of Religion were to cause much disquiet in the region from 1562 onwards. The town was successively captured and recaptured by Huguenots and Catholics. In 1590, Henry IV, the new protestant King of France, set siege before Falaise, which was held by the League, an ultra-Catholic movement that had refused to acknowledge his sovereignty. Thanks to its cannons, the royal army had no trouble in opening a breach in the castle ramparts and the stronghold was rapidly captured. The walls failed to resist the cannonballs of what had become a formidable artillery. This event symbolically marked the end of an era for Falaise Castle. It lost its defensive role and was relegated, which meant its removal from the list of fortresses to be maintained.

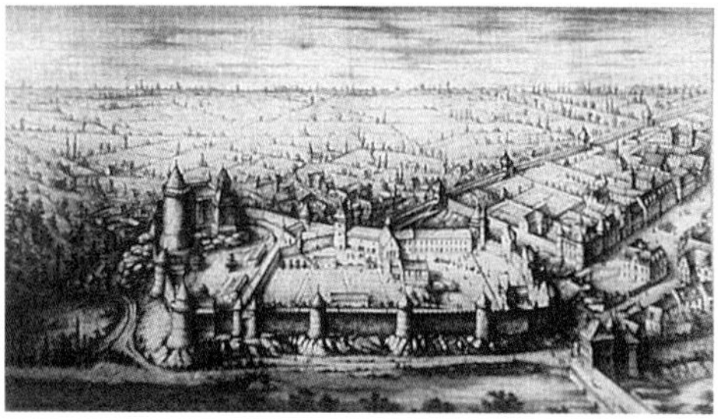

Falaise Castle in the 16th century, 19th century engraving by Trolonge, after an old print.
© Calvados Departmental Archives.

View of the castle in 1822 from the north-west. The school can be seen on the left. Engraving by J.S. Cotman. Architectural antiquities of Normandy, J. & A. Arch, London, 1822. Public domain.

Only a small garrison of sixty men was kept. The loss of the castle's military role can also be explained by the return of domestic peace which was guaranteed by absolute monarchy, conflict henceforth being concentrated on the kingdom's disputed frontiers. Various work campaigns, demolition in particular, were undertaken, including the razing of the tower and wall coping and the destruction of certain buildings within the enclosure. From the early 17th century onwards, the governor's lieutenant complained to the royal administration of the great state of dilapidation suffered by the castle's "houses".

In the early 18th century, the governor's position was bought by the Morell d'Aubigny family, who were among the local nobility and who thereafter could make use of the governor's dwelling, on the same basis as the medieval viscount's dwelling. The governor's office was finally shed in 1777. In 1772, the Count of Aubigny requested and obtained the king's permission to demolish the dilapidated castle chapel nave in order to recover the material and to use it to restore the choir. In his request, he mentioned "*the convenience of having mass at home*", but considered that "*the part of the choir is far sufficient to accommodate* [his] *family and* [his] *servants*". The keeps, which were still used as a prison until 1708, are represented as abandoned and partly in ruins on a plan of the enclosure dating from 1788. At this date, the fortified entrance gateway and the upper courtyard had disappeared. As had the many constructions that had characterised the lower courtyard since the Middle Ages, with the exception of the governor's dwelling and the choir of the St. Nicholas Chapel. They made way for gardens, created to adorn the governor's residence. The castle was of lesser importance to the town which was gradually modernised. Falaise was to see its very first urban planning campaign; a promenade planted with trees replaced the defensive Bercagnes pond. The inhabitants took possession of the ditches. During the French Revolution, the municipality planned to destroy the castle, before abandoning the idea. Instead, they decided to transform it into a prison and the establish the gendarmerie there. This project was also abandoned and, in 1803, the dwelling finally housed a high school.

Oblique view of Falaise in the 17th century.
Engraving by Mérian taken from Topographia Galliae, 1657. © Calvados Departmental Archives.

A seemingly formidable fortress

A striking description of the castle and the town dating from the 1590 siege provides us with evidence that, in the late 16th century, the stronghold remained daunting to its assailants, "His Majesty Henry IV arrived at the same time as the lord marshal de Biron on a reconnaissance mission of the said town and castle which are very good: the said town is enclosed by a great moat whose water cannot be rerouted, the walls are good, flanked with good towers and the outskirts presenting a barrier to the establishment of a battery; the castle is even better, equipped with large strong towers and the walls are very good, with a large and separate keep, dug with good and deep ditches [...]"

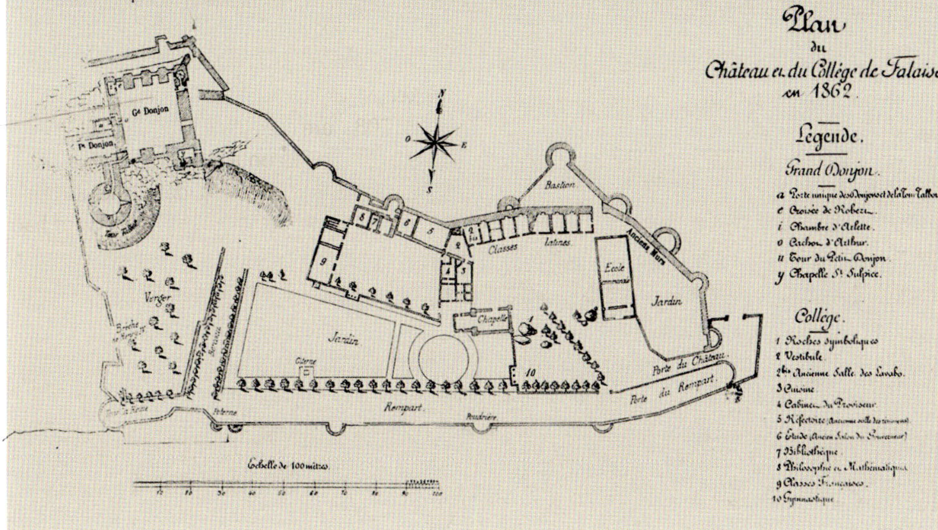

These two engravings illustrate the state of ruin of the castle keeps in the early 19th century. Engraving by Albert d'Oilliamson.
Pays de Falaise Media library / German Collection.

The 19th, 20th and 21st century restoration campaigns

From its foundation to the late Middle Ages, the castle was regularly improved in response to evolutions in siege warfare. The loss of its military use in the late 16th century led to a long period of decline. Although the presence of the last governors, then the school, within the castle enclosure spurred summary maintenance of the ramparts, the abandoned keeps gradually deteriorated.

For over twenty years, the castle has benefited from major restoration. This time, the aim was no longer to improve its defences, but to recreate best possible the fortified castle's medieval identity and purpose. This ambitious project was the result of the Falaise Town Council's great determination to give prominence to the monument. Since 1980, the town's successive mayors and their municipal teams have undertaken to totally restore the site. This rehabilitation has benefited from precious support from the Calvados Council, the Lower Normandy Regional Council and the Regional Directorate for Cultural Affairs (Ministry for Culture).

The restored Small Keep windows in the early 20th century. Old postcard, private collection.

One of the Great Keep windows in a state of ruin. 19th century engraving.

The Small Keep in the early 20th century. Old postcard, private collection.

Elevation plan of the castle from the south.
Illustration by Jean-Charles Danjoy, Historic Monuments architect, 1842. Photograph RMN, © J.-L. Paillé.

The 19th century

The first sign of revived interest in the castle dates from the early 19th century. Its romantic ruin aspect inspired artists who produced many drawings, engravings and paintings of the site. Their works offer us an insight into the state of the constructions prior to the first restoration work. Concurrently, antique dealers and emerging learned societies, who began to study old monuments, paid particular attention to Falaise Castle. Their enthusiasm was parallel to increasing national awareness of the heritage value of historic buildings, in reaction to excessive revolutionary vandalism. The position of Inspector of Historic Monuments was created in 1830, followed by the Historic Monuments Commission in 1837. In 1840, the castle was placed on the first "list of monuments for which safeguard operations are requested" due to its historic importance and to the worrying state of the keeps. Its inscription enabled the castle to benefit from the first protective measures and to associated grants: restoration work could begin.

The first work on the keeps was entrusted to the architect Jean-Charles Danjoy in 1842. He drew up the very first accurate plans of the castle and proposed a large-scale restoration campaign: elimination of overgrown vegetation, repair of stonework on the Great Keep – the most threatened, reconstruction of one of its twin windows based on the same model as similar existing windows, restoration of window vaults, stairs and the *capella* and weatherproofing of walls. Only a small part of the planned work was actually carried out. The architect, who was on bad terms with the local authorities and his superiors, abandoned the project in 1845.

In 1863, resumption of work was entrusted to Victor Ruprich-Robert, a Historic Monument architect who based his restoration project for the three keeps on a painstaking historic and architectural study. Work conducted from 1864 to 1870 durably preserved the stonework of the Great Keep. Paradoxically, restoration work concealed any trace of the original structure. We know nothing of the type of roofing, flooring or partitioning that existed within the Norman keeps before their collapse: their ruins were cleared and dispersed without being studied. The keep remained an empty shell. A gallery installed against the inside walls of the first floor offered access to the windows, the chapel and offered views of the lower portions of the edifice. This arrangement bore witness to the town's desire to attract tourists around the emerging theme of monumental tourism.

Detail of one of the Great Keep's capitals.
Illustration by Jean-Charles Danjoy. Photograph RMN, © J.-L. Paillé.

The Small Keep and the Talbot Tower were restored according to Victor Ruprich-Robert's original plan, drafted in the early 20th century, by his son, Gabriel Ruprich-Robert, assisted by Trolonge, the municipal architect.

South facade of the Great Keep and Talbot Tower.
Illustration by Jean-Charles Danjoy, Historic Monuments architect. Photograph RMN, © J.-L. Paillé.

The school built against the north rampart and, to the left, the 12th century castle chapel.
Old postcard, private collection.

The ruins of the school after the bombardments.
Falaise Town Council.

The 20th century

The former school buildings housed the "complementary hospital n°11". It was partly reserved for use by Muslim soldiers. In 1940, the castle was requisitioned by the occupant who installed its supply corps services for the troops posted in the region. In the summer of 1944, both the town and the castle suffered severe damage following aerial bombardments and ground-based combat during the Battle of Normandy. On the 12th of August 1944, some of the Allied bombs, whose target was Boulevard des Bercagnes, landed on the castle. The east and south ramparts were damaged. The school buildings were almost totally destroyed. The choir of the St. Nicholas Chapel was annihilated. However, the conflict left the keeps virtually intact.

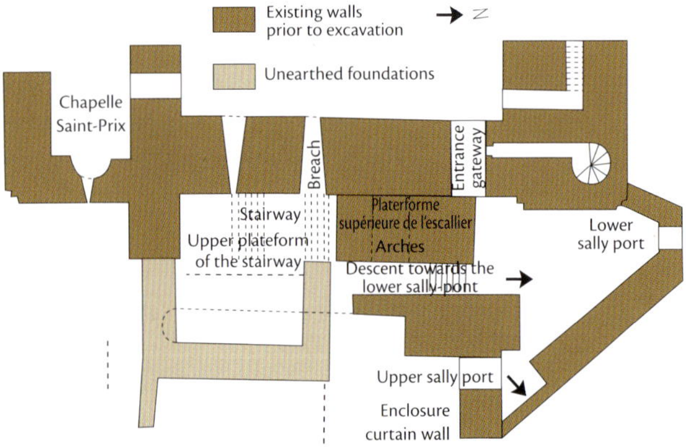

Forebuilding excavation plan dating from 1948 /
Illustration by Doctor Doranlo / Falaise Town Council

The post-war years

From 1948 to 1958, the chief architects, Maurice Berry and Jean Merlet took on the repair of the breaches in the ramparts and supervised clearing of the enclosure and the keeps. The vestiges of the school building were deemed to be of no architectural or historic interest and were, consequently, destroyed. Only the medieval windows in the north rampart and the Neoclassical arcades of the governor's dwelling were preserved to bear witness to the existence of former houses. Today, these vestiges are part of the Visitor's centre. The keeps had benefited from no repair whatsoever since the beginning of the century: the east facade of the Great Keep, the gaps in which had been hastily filled in the 19th century, was in a sad state of dilapidation. It was only in 1948 that the first archaeological excavation was organised within the castle, under the direction of Dr. Raoul Doranlo. In the upper courtyard, the operation unveiled the foundations of a rectangular edifice at the foot of the Great Keep. The construction, established parallel

The same site after construction of the visitor's centre in 2003. Falaise Town Council.

to the facade, is identified as a forebuilding whose purpose was to defend access to the keep.

1986 – 1996: restoration of the keeps

In 1980, in an aim to improve the castle's tourist appeal, the Falaise Town Council called upon the Chief Architect of Historic Monuments, Bruno Decaris, to develop a project to restore the keeps. Work began in 1986 and lasted ten years. The aim was, in particular, to reproduce the interior arrangements and movements of the Great and the Small Keeps - hitherto impossible for deprived of their floors and ceilings. The lack of sources on missing features excluded any possibility of restoring to produce a replica of the original state. In locations where no trace remained of former installations, the architect marked his intervention with a resolutely contemporary architectural style. His aim was to evoke the missing features without pretence and to restore the monument's clarity. The project conformed with the conservation guidelines set down by the Venice Charter of 1964 put forward by Unesco and adopted in France. The Charter states that "the process of restoration is a highly specialised operation" and that, "it must stop at the point where conjecture begins... Any extra work which is indispensable must be distinct from the architectural composition and must bear a contemporary stamp". It was important to avoid the error of trying to interpret the vestiges, which can lead to pastiches which may confuse visitors over what is "genuinely old" and what is "imitation".

The keep during the restoration campaign by Bruno Decaris: installation of the perimetral roof beams.
Photograph by B. Decaris. Falaise Town Council.

The keeps during restoration by Bruno Decaris.
Photograph by B. Decaris. Falaise Town Council.

Installation of the three-dimensional structures which support the floor of the *aula*.
Photograph by B. Decaris. Falaise Town Council.

Teflon roofing on the Great Keep.
Photograph by F. Trouillet. Falaise Town Council.

The Talbot Tower after the 1944 bombings. Falaise Town Council.

Restoration of the Talbot Tower in 1986-1987. Photograph by B. Decaris. Falaise Town Council.

1986 – 1987: Restoration of the Talbot Tower

Although it had benefited from better maintenance than the Norman keeps, the Talbot Tower nevertheless required major renovation. During the same campaign, the vaults and the flooring of its different levels were restored; the top of the tower was arranged in order to enable visitors to safely admire the panorama it offers; the outside walls were renovated and adorned with a levelling plaster coat.

1992-1996: restoration of the Anglo-Norman keeps

The type and dimensions of the original roofing are unknown. Only the supporting wall, the base of which remains, separating the *aula* from the *camera*, offers an insight into the length and the orientation of the associated roof timbers. To evoke their presence, the architect chose Teflon roofing supported by a metallic frame, the overall aspect of which is somewhat reminiscent of tents. In the *aula*, a particularly ostentatious room during the 12th century, the floor has been reproduced using glass and lead slabs, on a self-supported metal frame. The elegance of the flooring reminds us of the great luxury of this room. The use of metal and glass, noble materials, is evocative of its aristocratic status. In the *camera* and the Small Keep, lead plates have been placed on a concrete slab. The windows have been

The restored Talbot Tower. Photograph F. Trouillet. Falaise Town Council.

Small Keep: recreation of the access stairway from the Great Keep. Photograph by Rochereau. Falaise Town Council.

The restored *aula* in the Great Keep. Photograph by Rochereau. Falaise Town Council.

The Norman keep at Castle Rising. The forebuilding that protects the entrance can clearly be seen in the centre. Courtesy of Castle Rising (Norfolk, England).

The forebuilding. Falaise Town Council.

glazed with intricately worked glass, whilst the inside walls are whitewashed. Both the visitor's imagination and sensitivity actively participate in the overall appreciation of the restored edifice.

1996: creation of the forebuilding

Work was completed with the reconstruction of the forebuilding, based on the results of archaeological excavation in 1948 and on the study of similar buildings, still in a preserved state on either side of the English Channel. Bruno Decaris drew particular inspiration from the forebuilding of Castle Rising keep, the architecture of which is very close to that of Falaise's Great Keep. Failing sufficient data, the architect opted for a modern recreation of the edifice's lost volumes. The chosen materials, concrete and metal, highlight the defensive purpose of the original building. In principal, Bruno Decaris' intervention is perfectly in keeping with the guidelines set down by the Venice Charter in that it reproduces a powerful reference to the Great Keep's former identity. In reality, Decaris' contribution proved to be a source of considerable controversy. The material he used – grey concrete – was criticised for its disheartening aspect, along with certain anachronistic details such as the entrance drawbridge and the loopholes.

Interior view of the forebuilding at Castle Rising. Courtesy of Castle Rising (Norfolk, England).

Interior of the forebuilding by Bruno Decaris. Photograph by B. Decaris. Falaise Town Council.

The 21st century

1998-2003: architectural intervention within the castle enclosure

In 1998, the town council requested that two new restoration projects be initiated by the new chief architect of Historic Monuments for Calvados, Daniel Lefèvre: restoration of the north rampart, required to enable the construction of a visitor's centre on the site of the former viscount's dwelling, and restoration of the upper courtyard fortifications. Prior archaeological studies inspired both campaigns.

For the upper courtyard, once defended by two curtain walls and a fortified entrance gateway, only part of the north tower remained and reconstruction as faithful as possible to the original arrangement was requested. The architect evoked the lost south curtain wall by creating a wall of dry stones contained within gabions. He used the same technique to mark the site and the circular plan of the entrance gateway's south tower. Finally, for crossing the ditch, he opted for an ultra-modern suspended walkway, failing formal identification of the former bridge piers upon which his construction could have been supported. The defensive ditch separating the lower and the upper yards was partially hollowed out.

The upper courtyard during restoration from 2001 to 2004. Falaise Town Council.

The Porte Saint-Nicolas gateway after restoration. Photograph by M. Dilys. Falaise Town Council.

2007-2015: the ramparts

Initiated in 2005, the "rampart" project marked the conclusion of work undertaken for over twenty years in order to improve and promote the castle. The project was, once more, entrusted to Daniel Lefèvre. Restoration work involved the ramparts in their entirety, together with the enclosure towers and the ditch on the town side, in order to recreate as far as possible the monument's defensive nature. The project did not aim to recreate the lost elevations but rather to consolidate existing vestiges. Only the partly collapsed west rampart was rebuilt to completely seal the enclosure. The walkways created alongside the ramparts invite visitors to discover the curtain walls and the enclosure towers. The general aim of this long restoration campaign was to restore the site's defensive character - work involving the ramparts, the enclosure towers and the ditch in front of the rampart on the town side. The rampart restoration benefited from systematic archaeological surveillance. Collected data was taken into account, step by step, and the architect's project was suitably adapted. Such data has also offered us improved understanding of the site's chronology and of its architectural evolution.

Since 2013, visitors can follow a trail associating traditional tour interpretation – explanatory panels, videos, furniture reproductions - and digital images. Permanent visual equipment installed within the enclosure offers different views of the lower courtyard as it may have appeared around the year 1160, at the peak of Anglo-Norman power. The tour of the keeps can be enhanced via the use of touchscreen tablets which offer spectacular reproductions of the former interior arrangements thanks to augmented reality. The application also includes a wealth of complementary contents to offer visitors an in-depth discovery of the site's history.

The restored upper courtyard: reminiscent of lost fortifications. Falaise Town Council.

The castle in the 18th century.
Falaise Town Council.